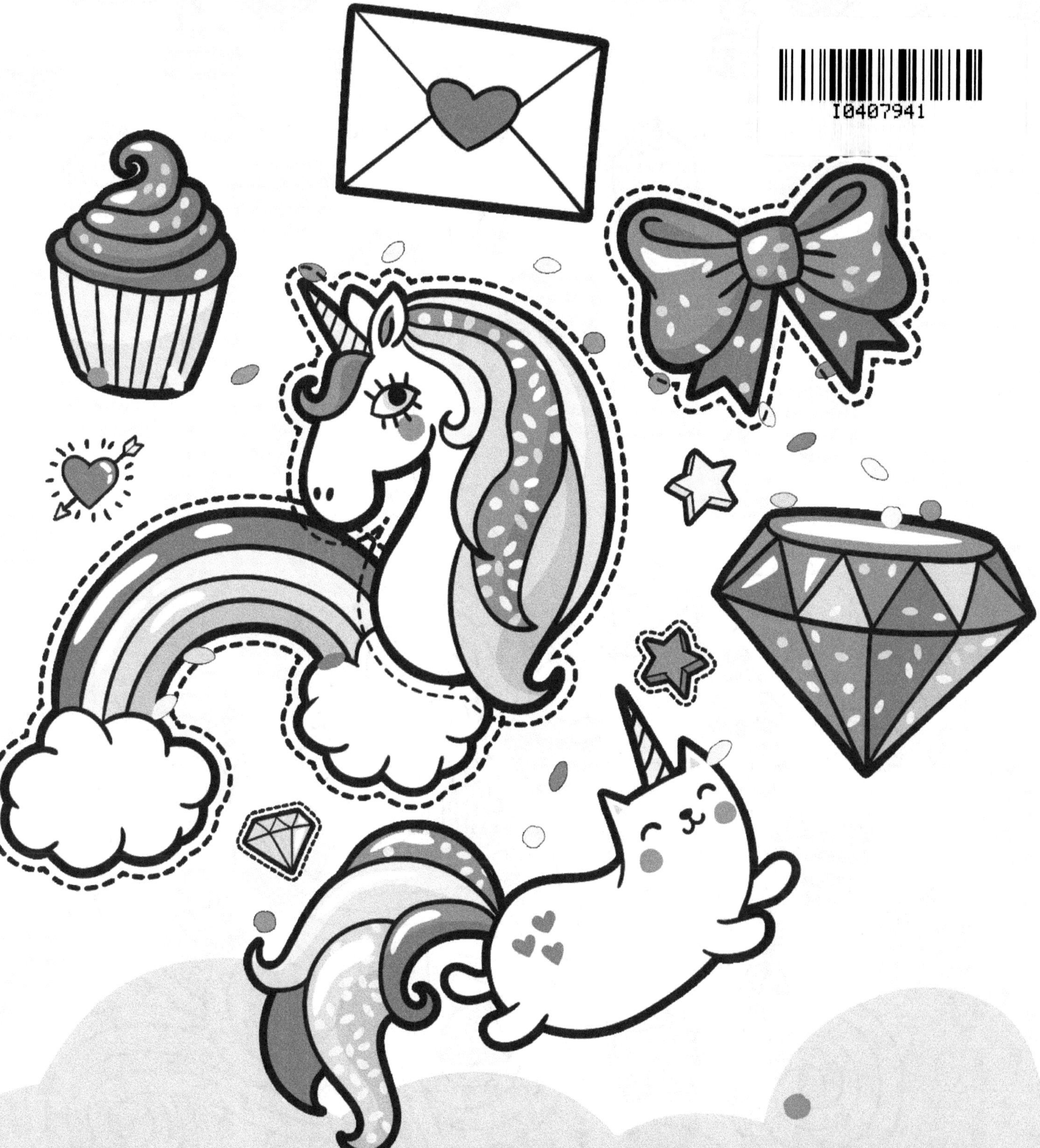

COLORING BOOKS *for Girls*

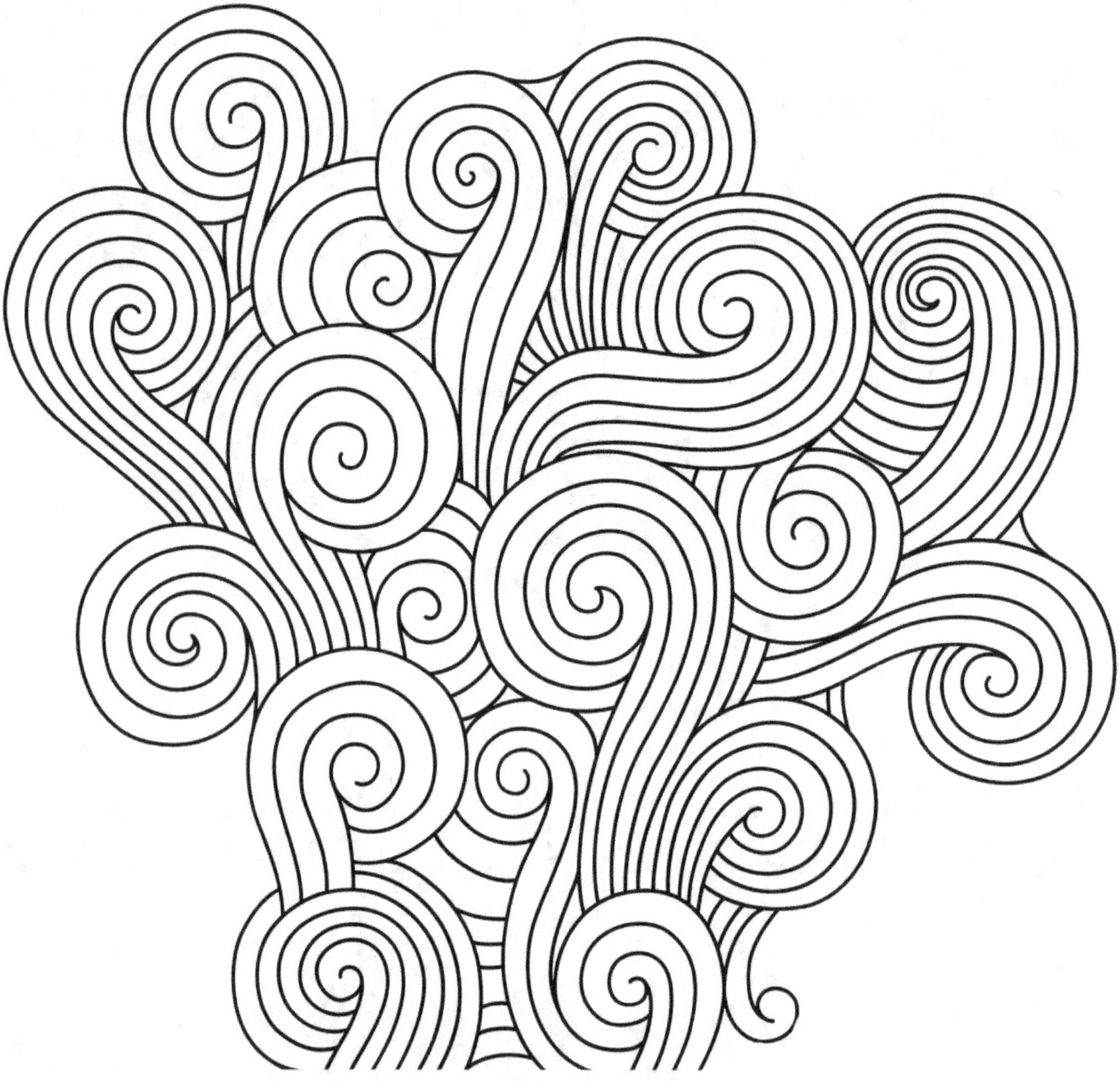

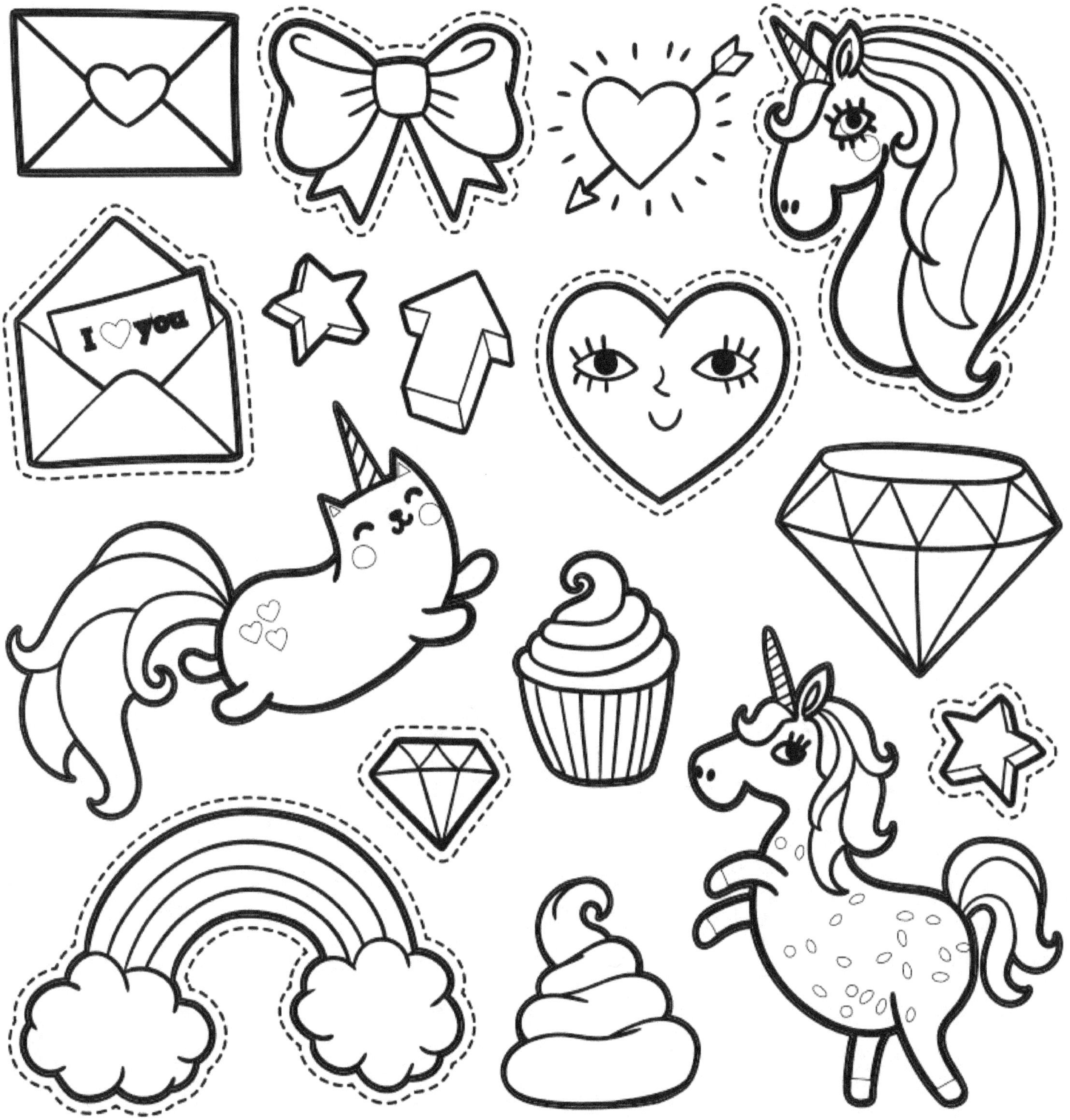
I ♡ you

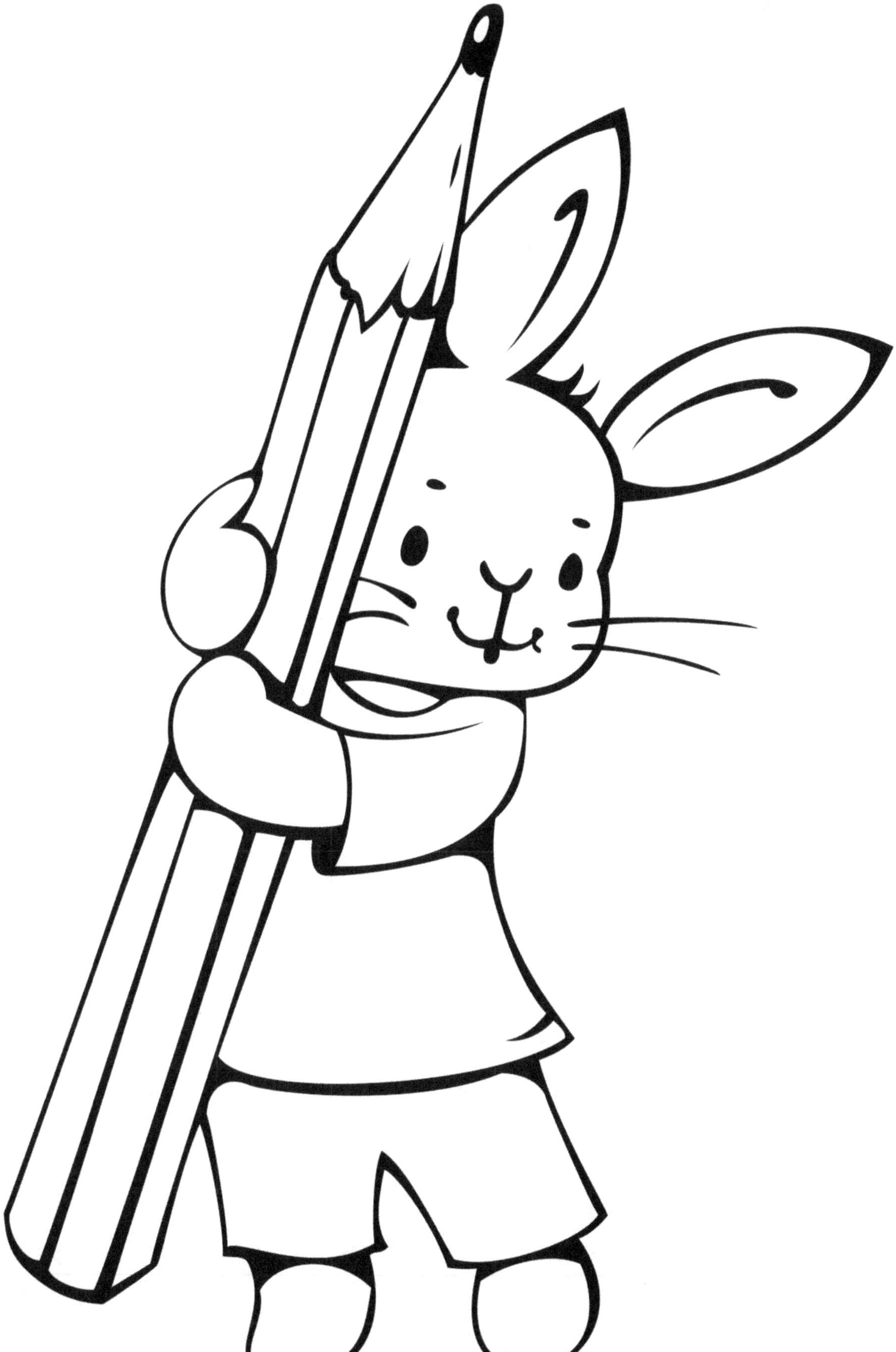

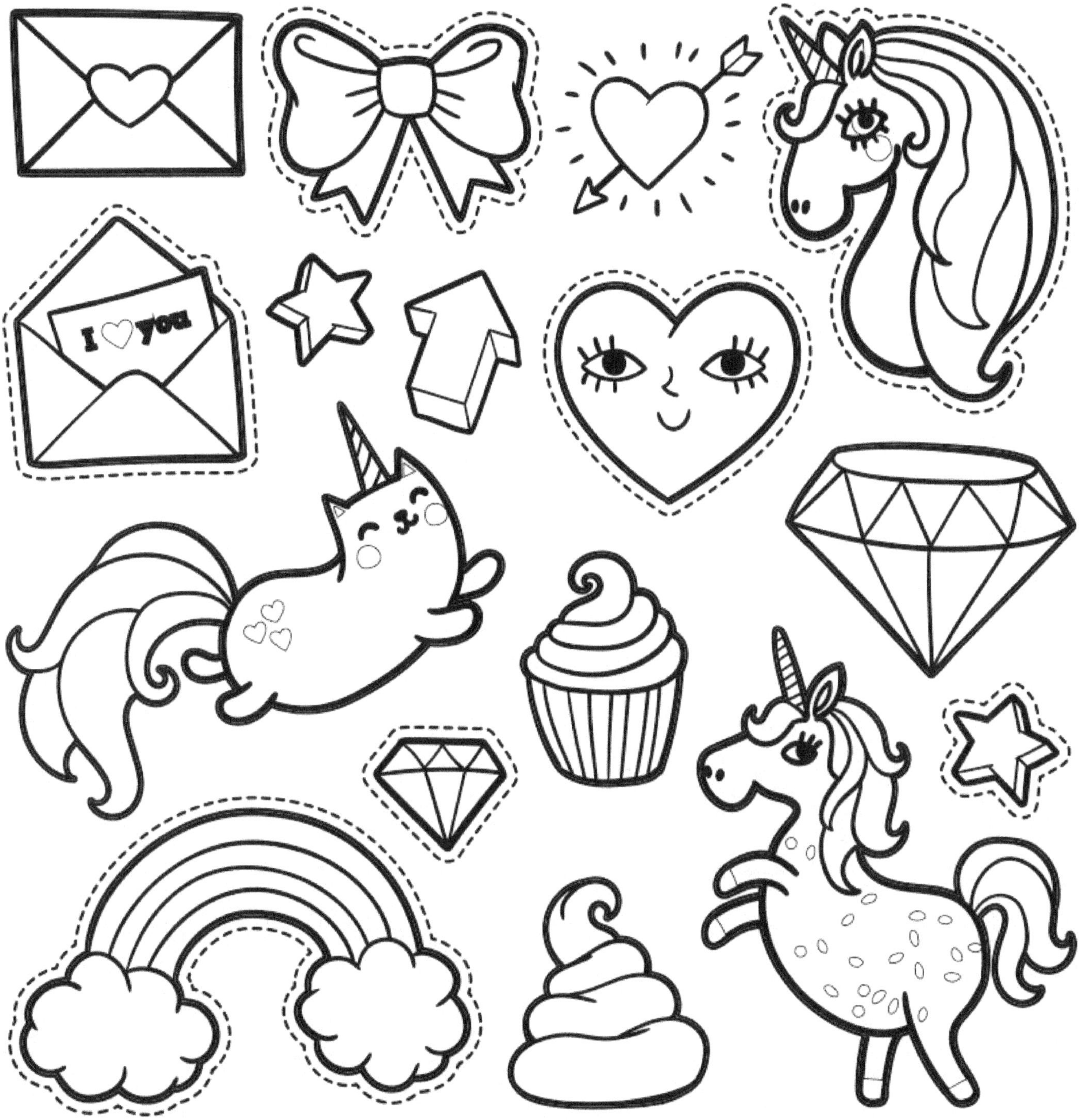
I ♡ you

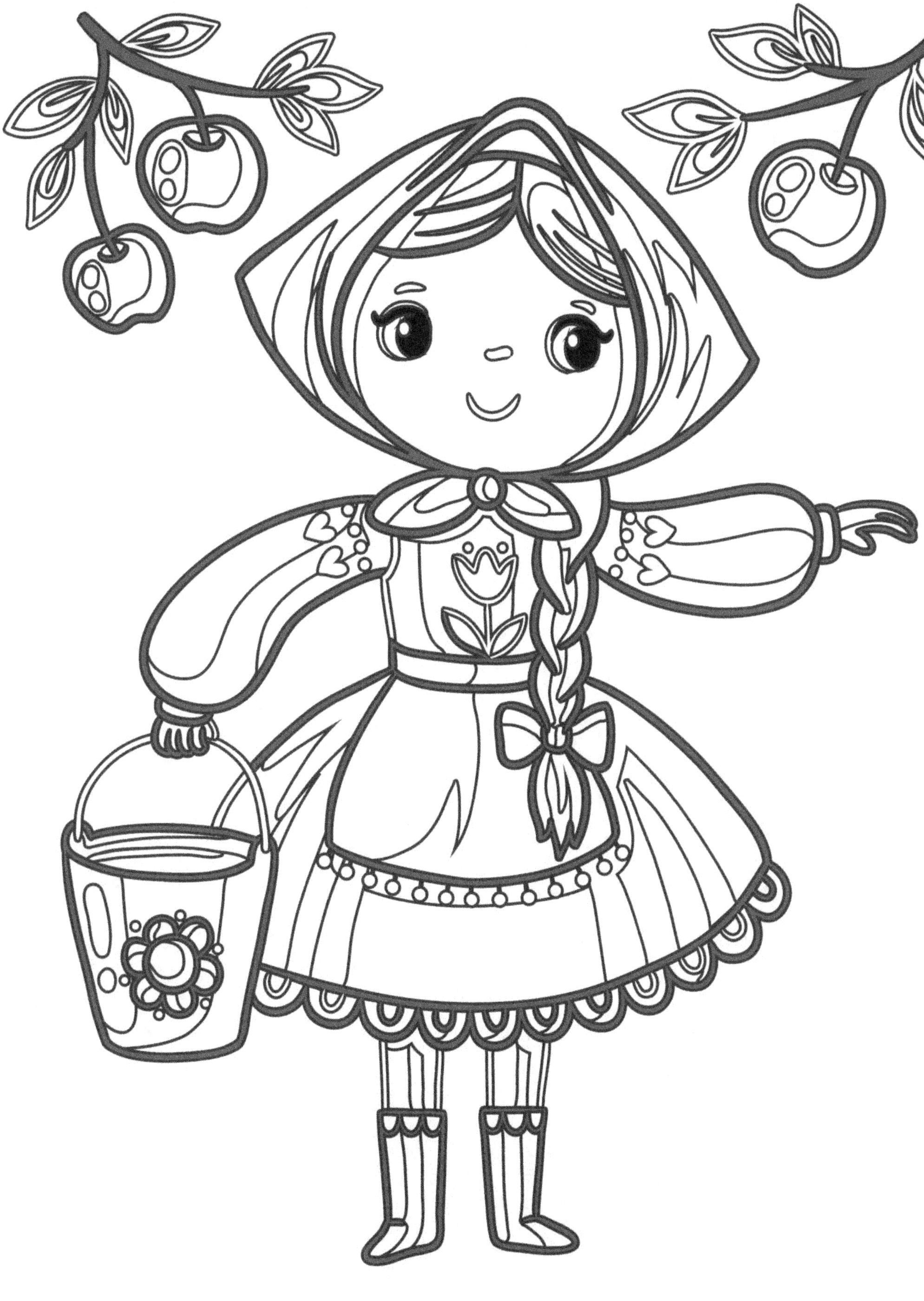

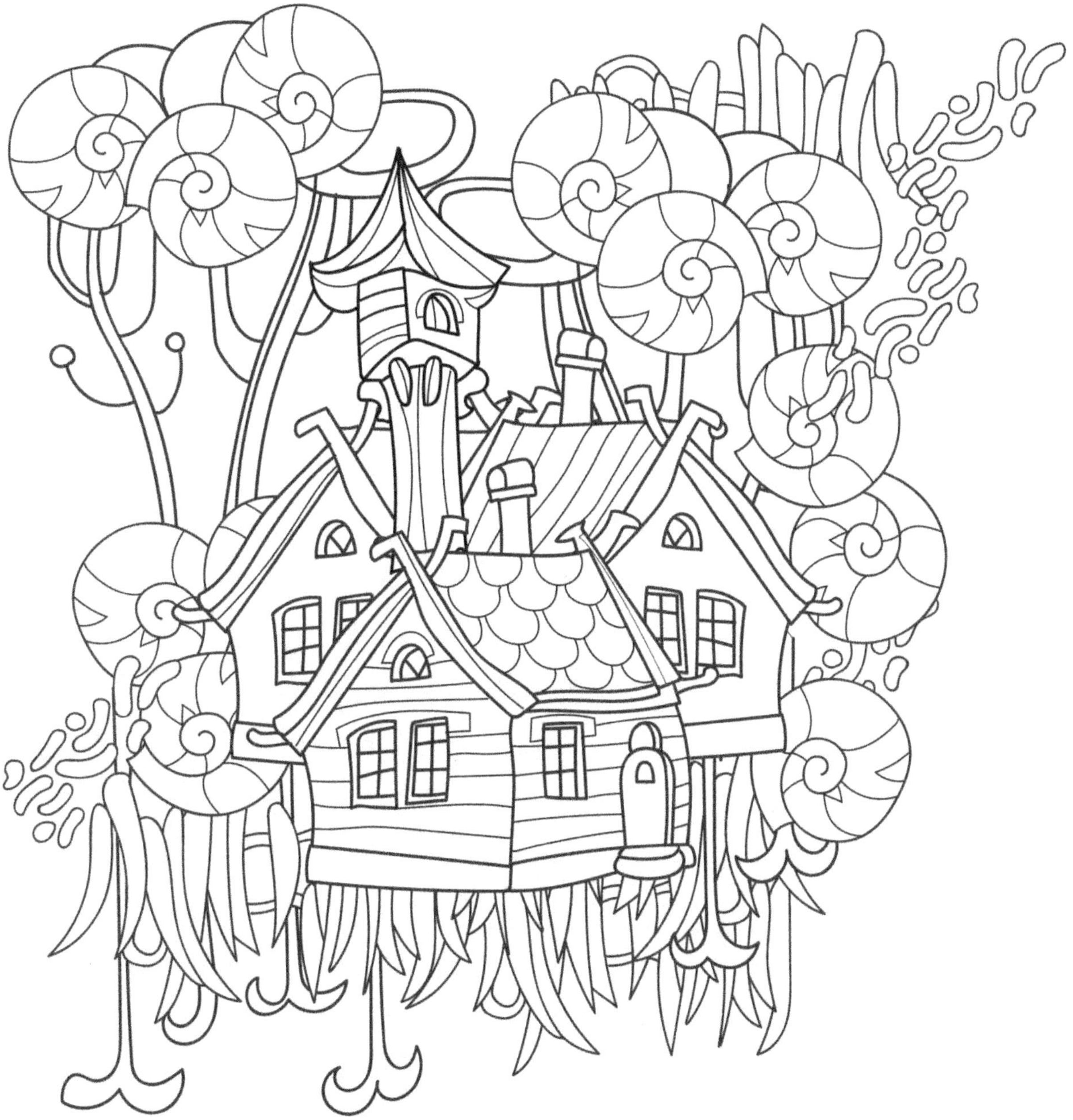

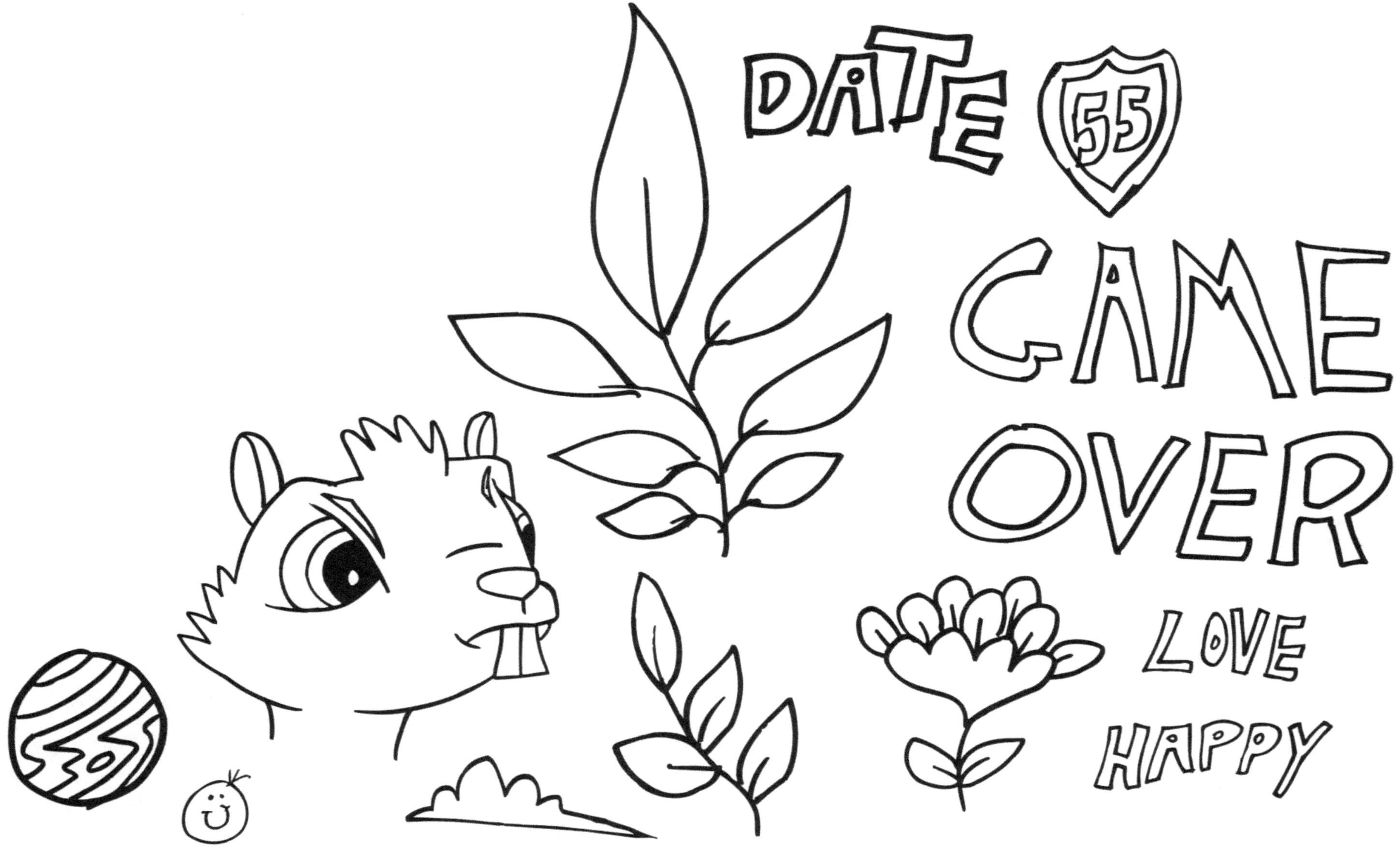
DATE
55
GAME
OVER
LOVE
HAPPY

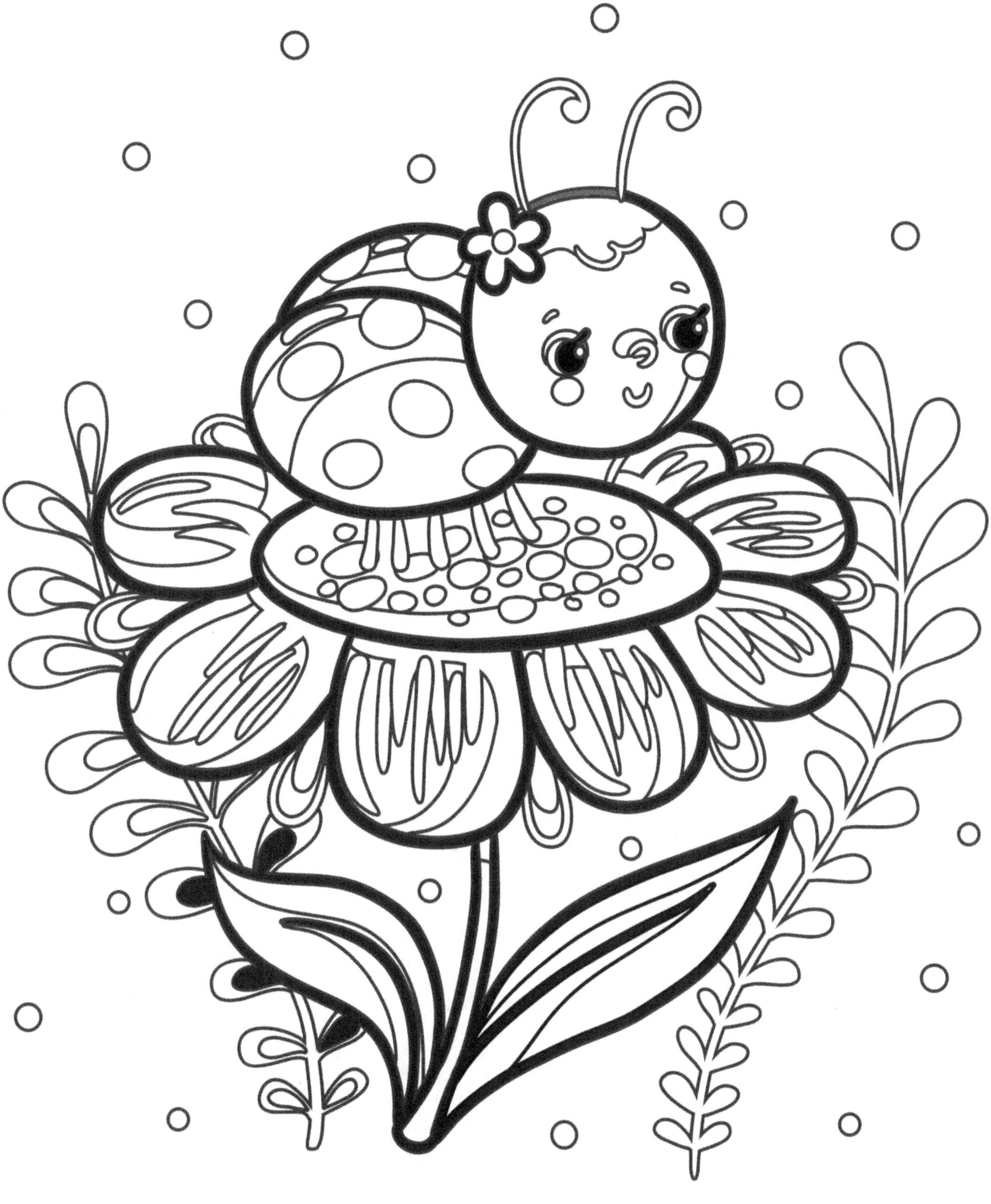

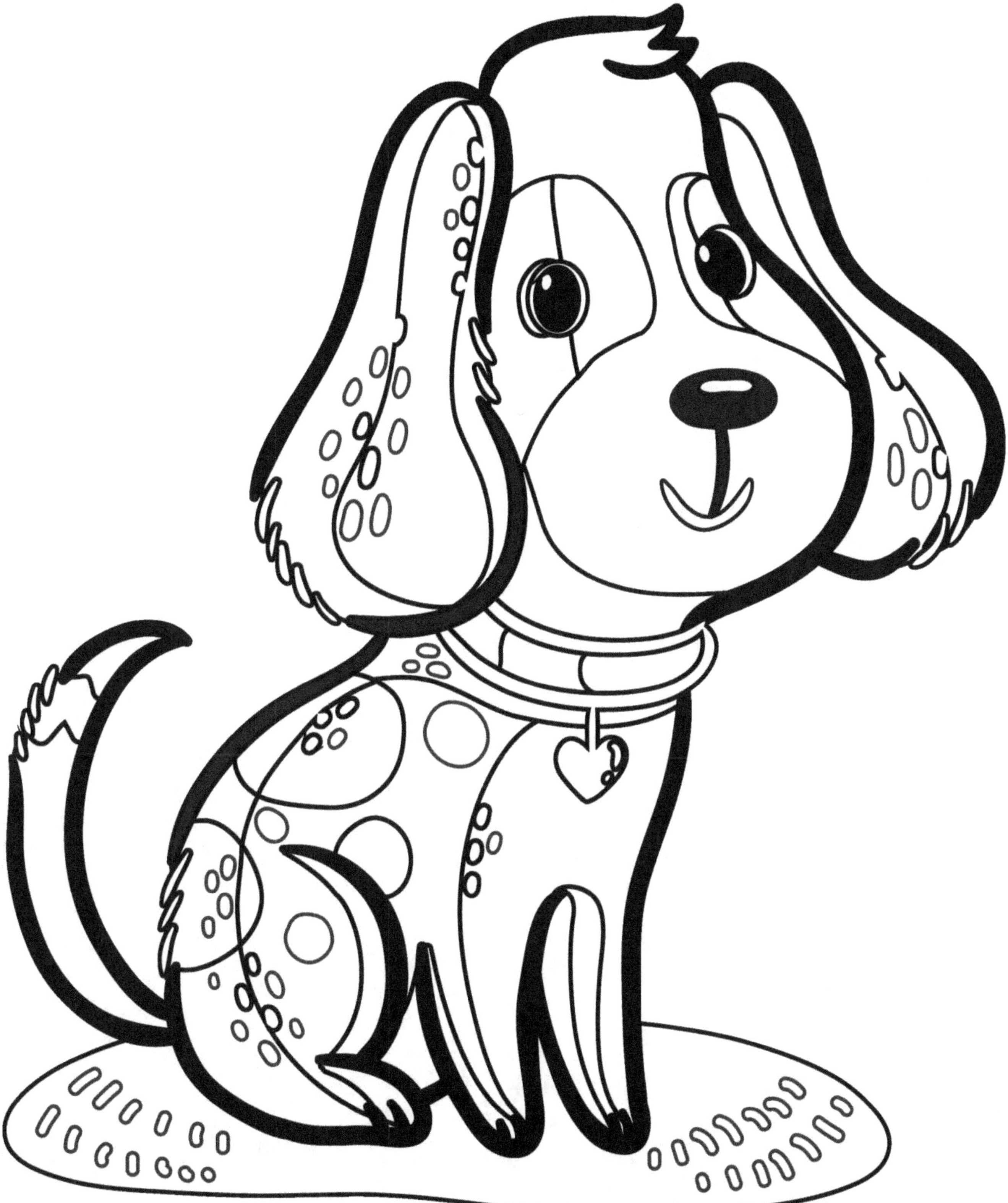

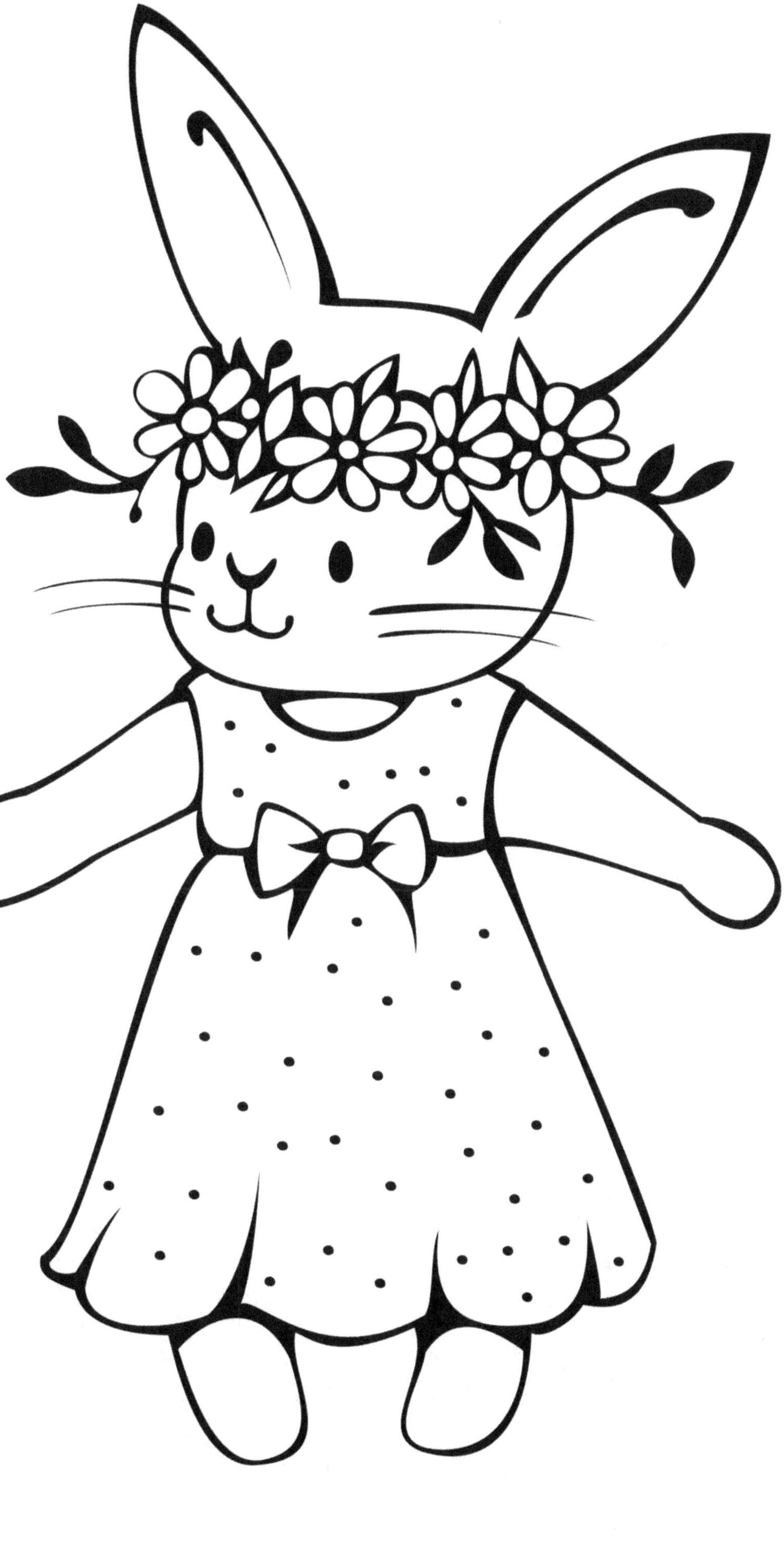

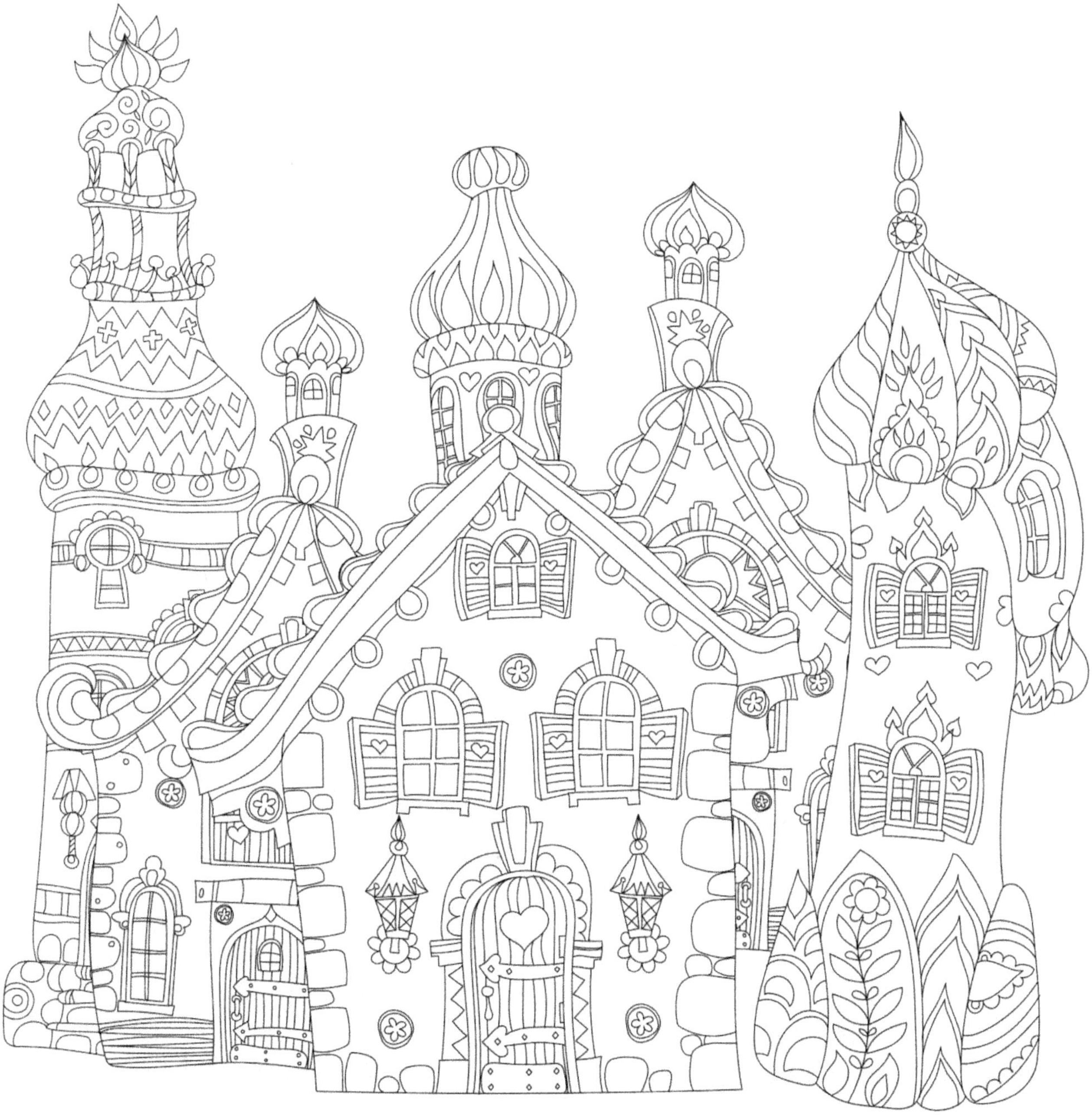

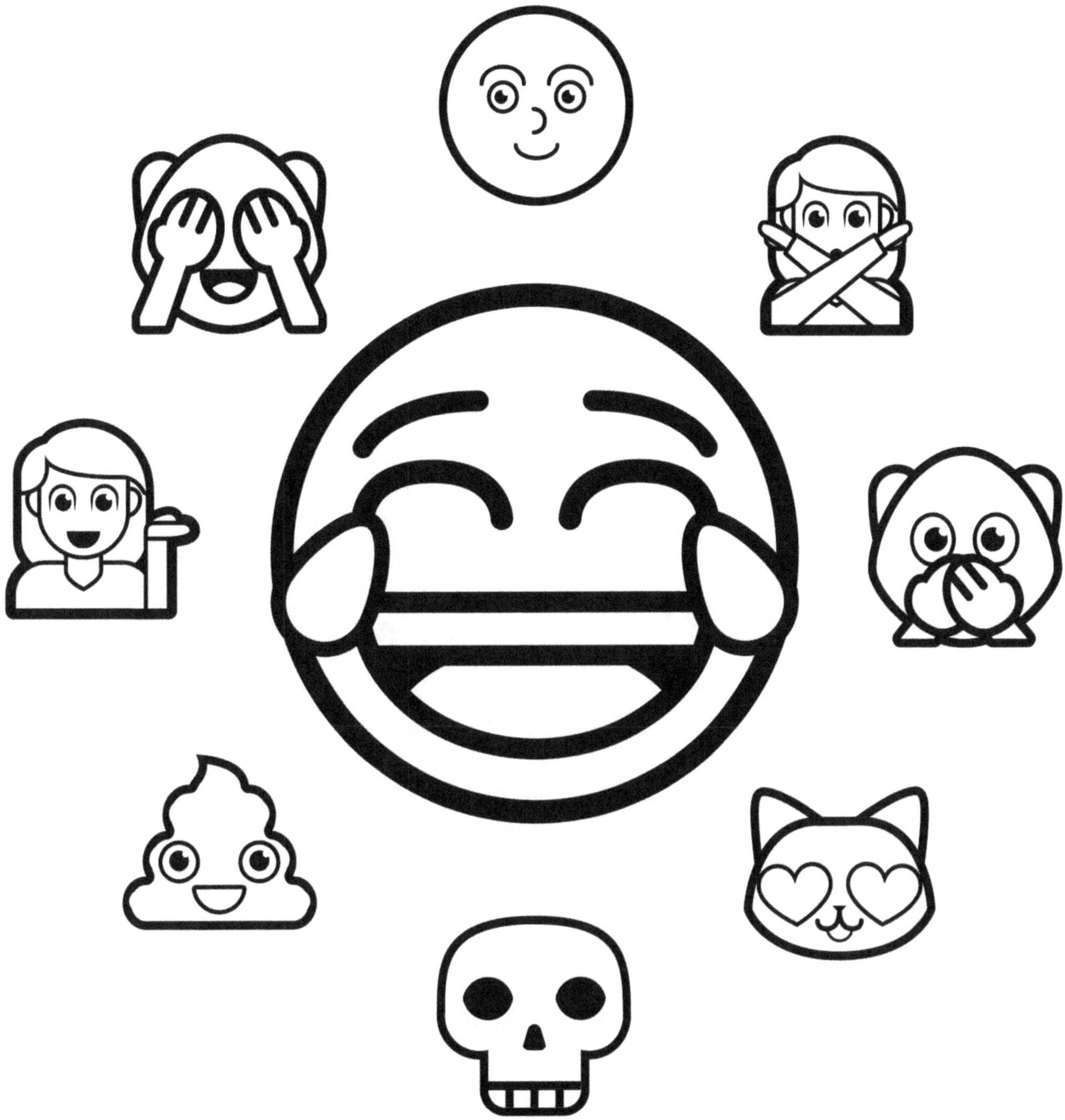

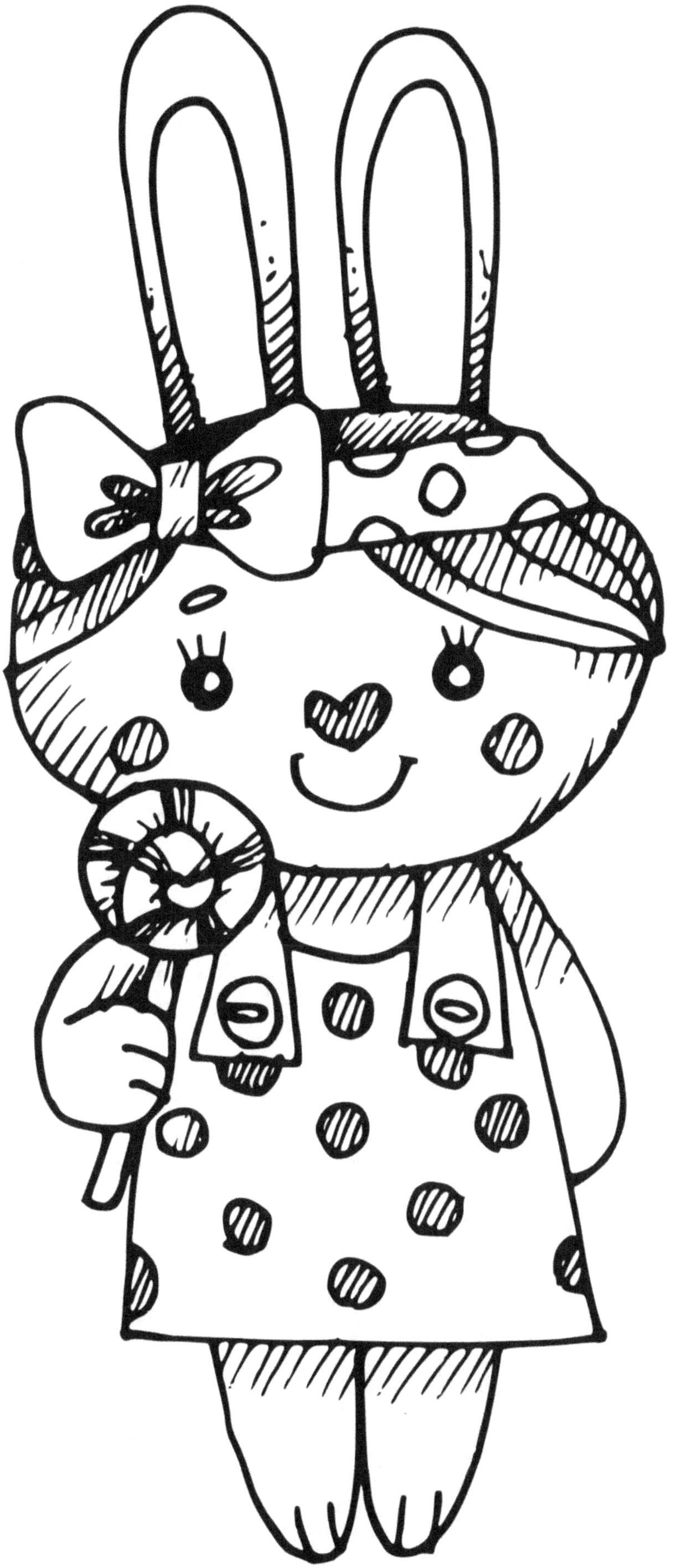

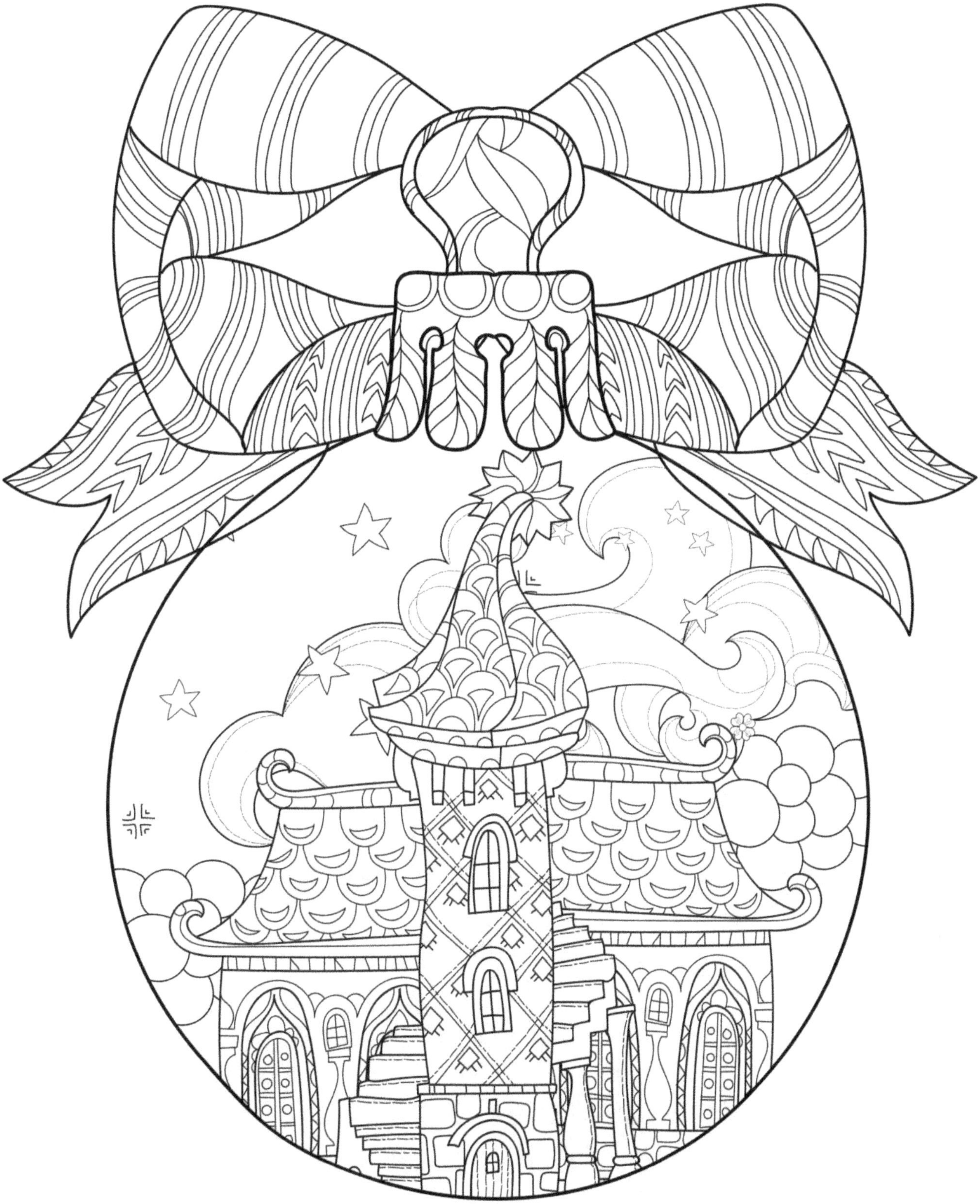

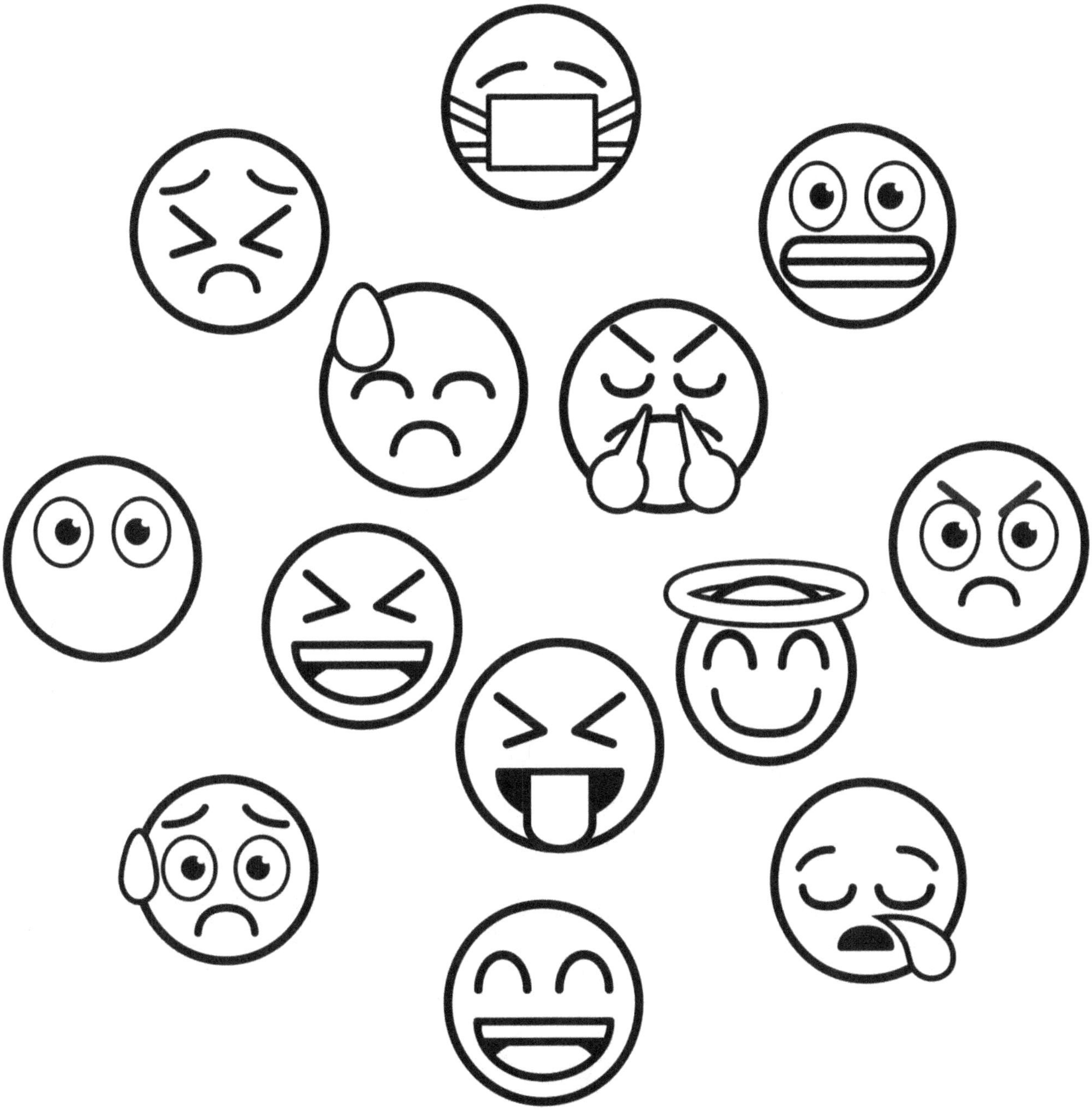

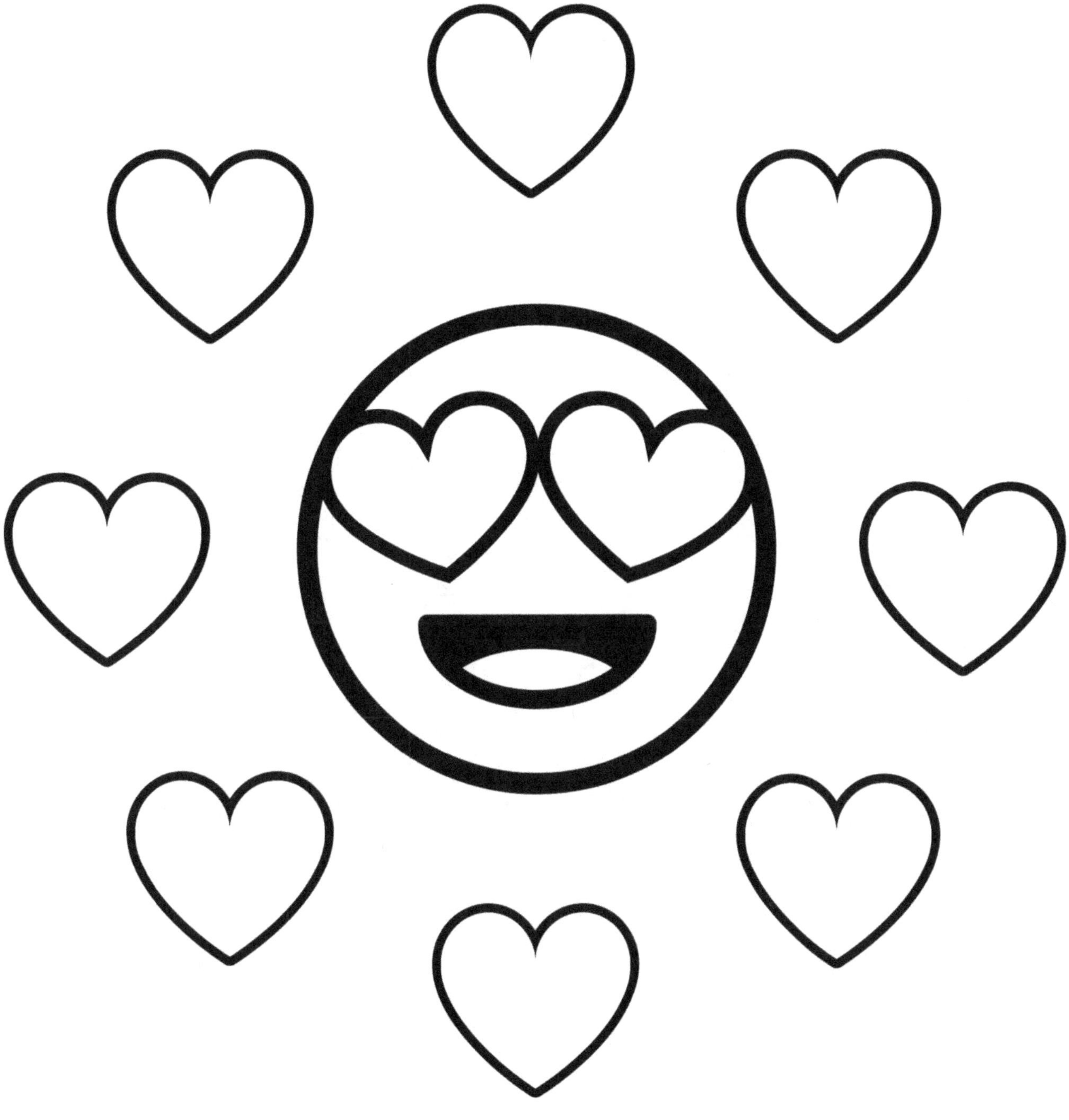

WOW!

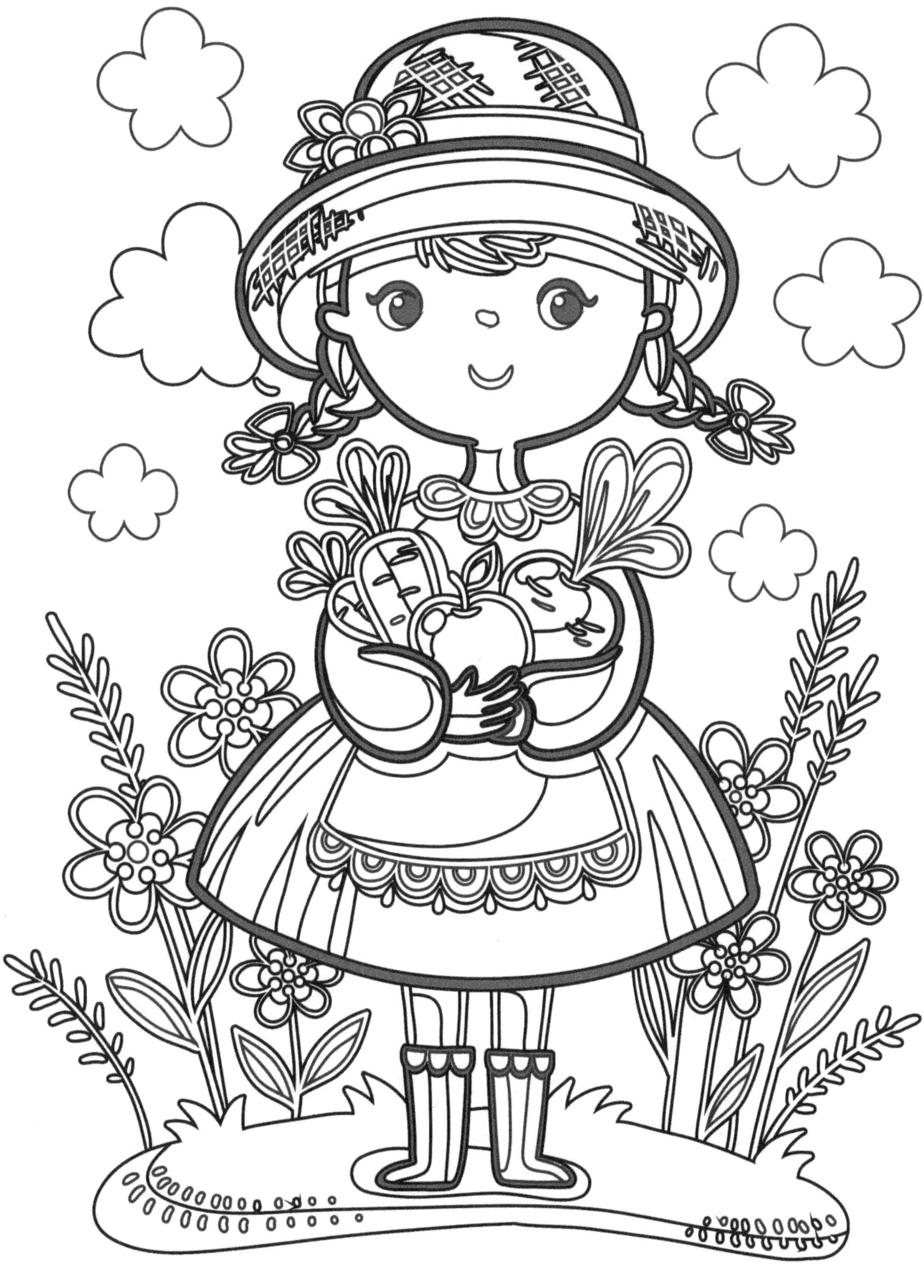

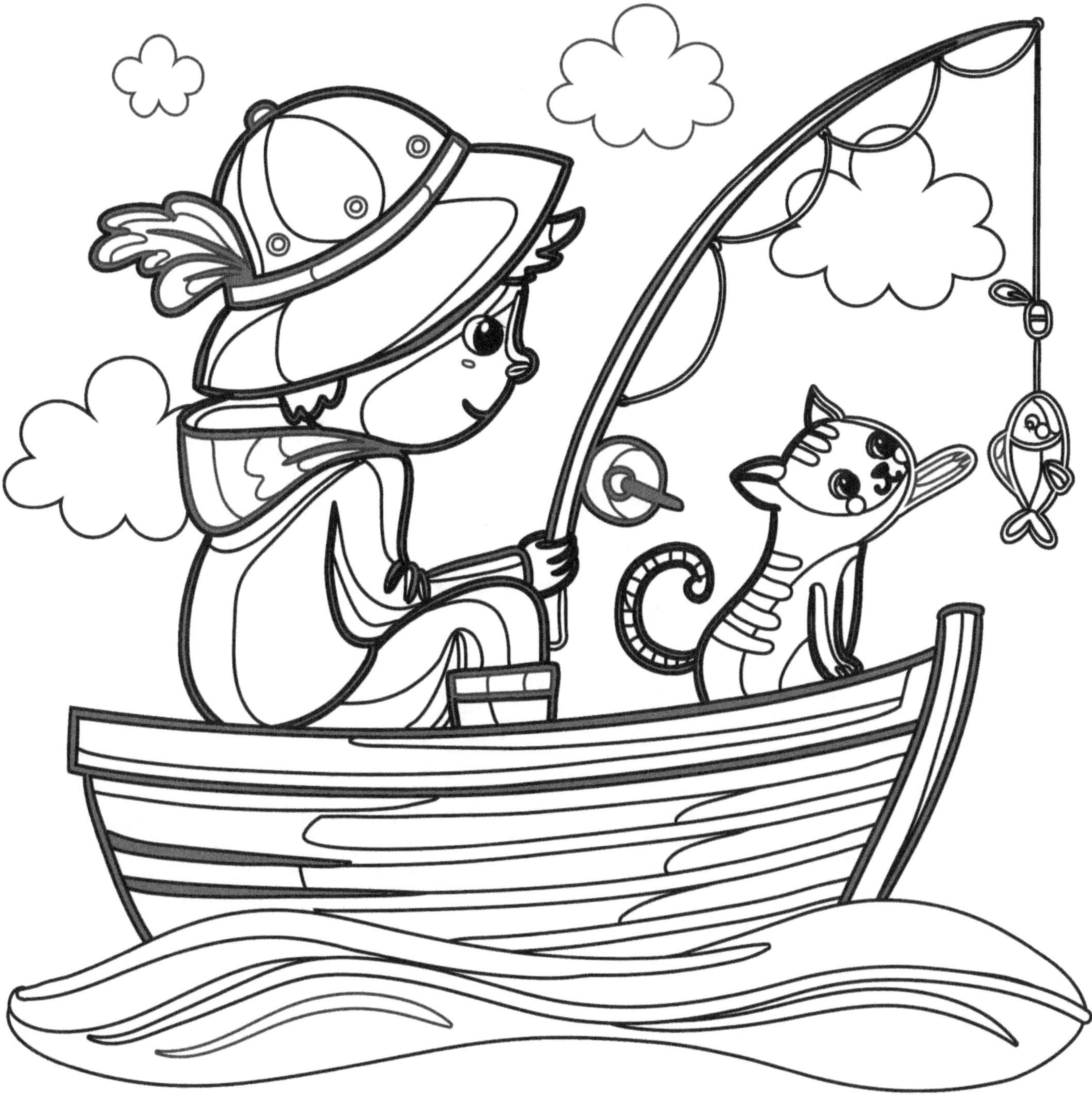

I ♥ U!

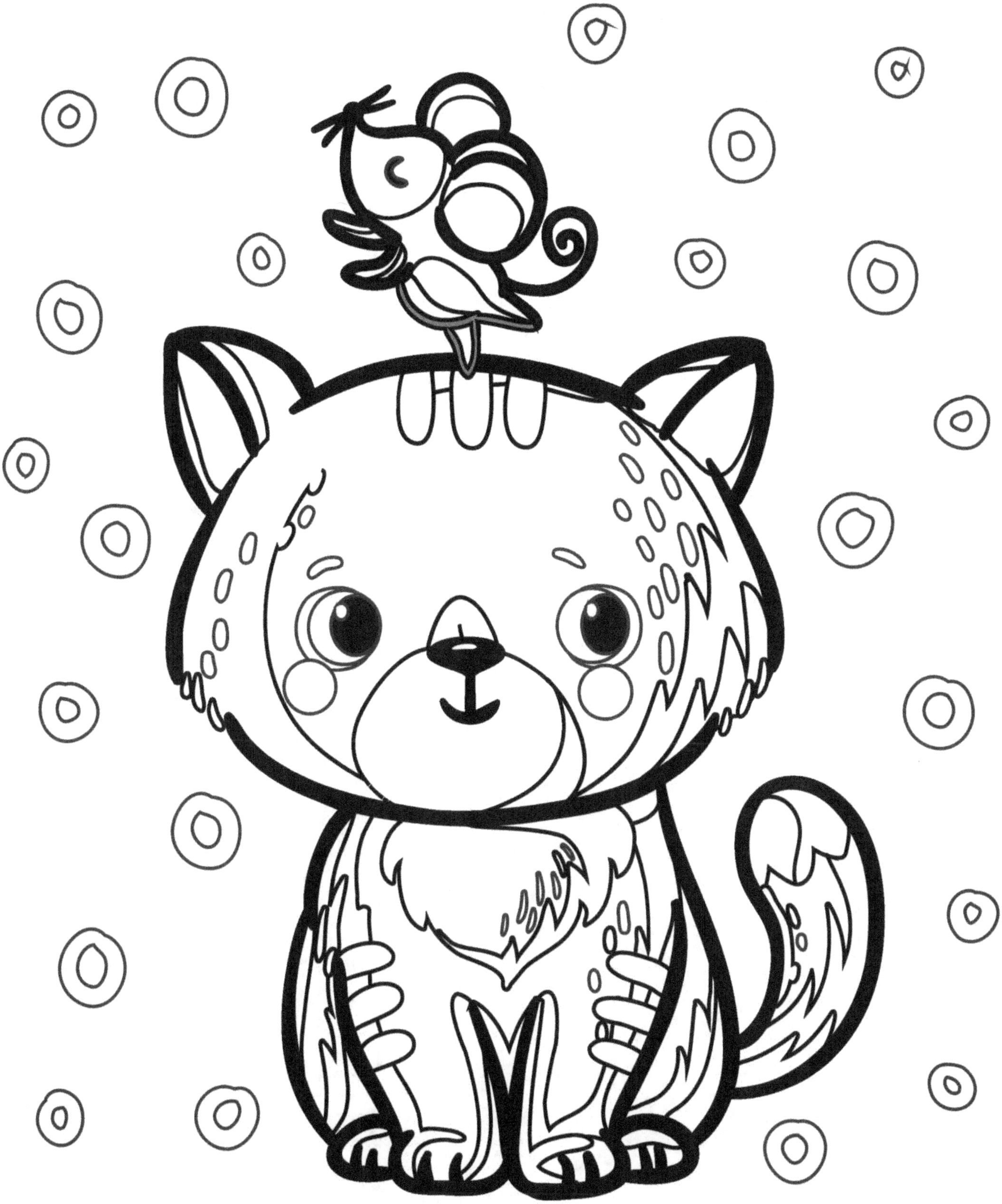

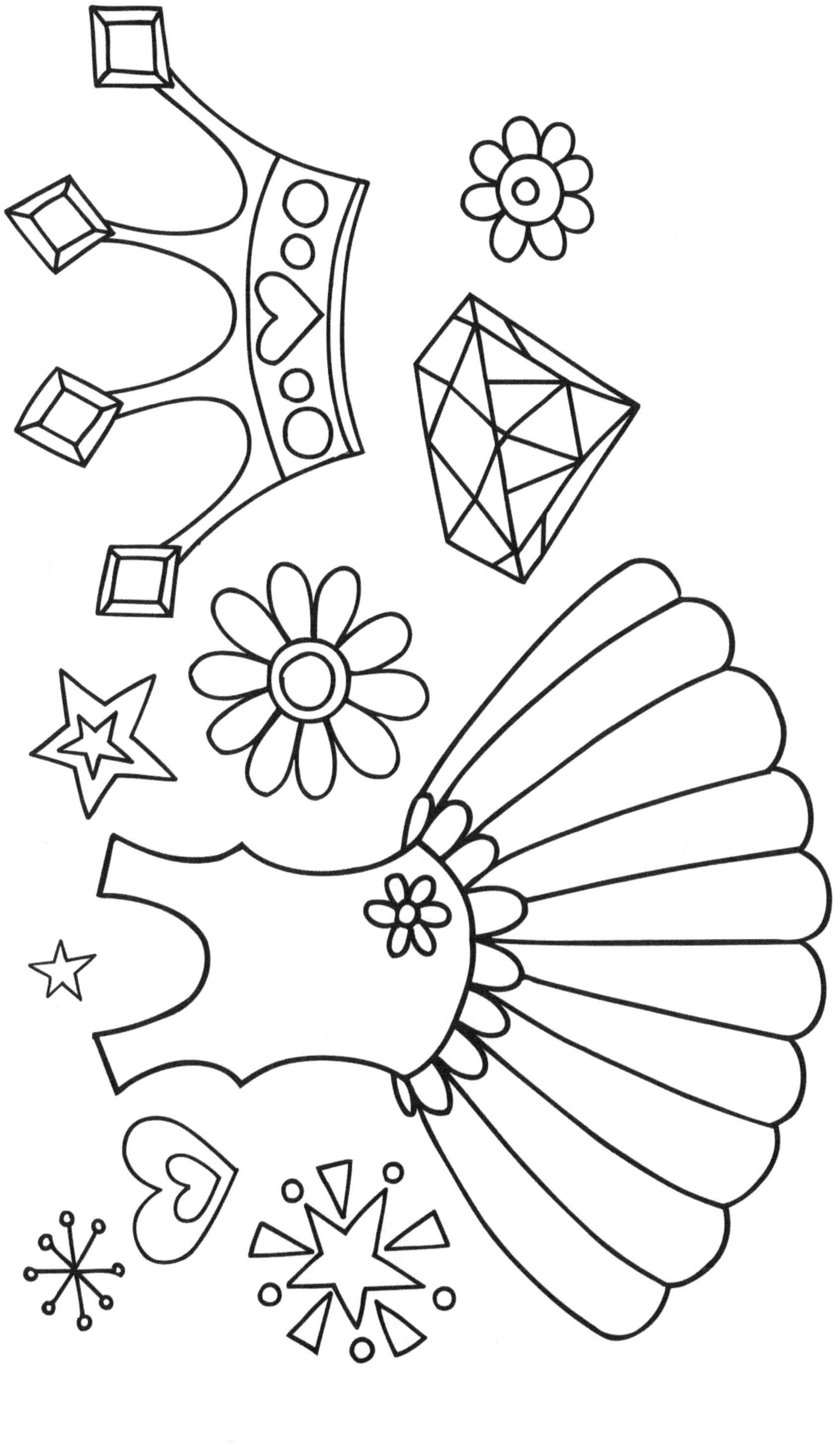

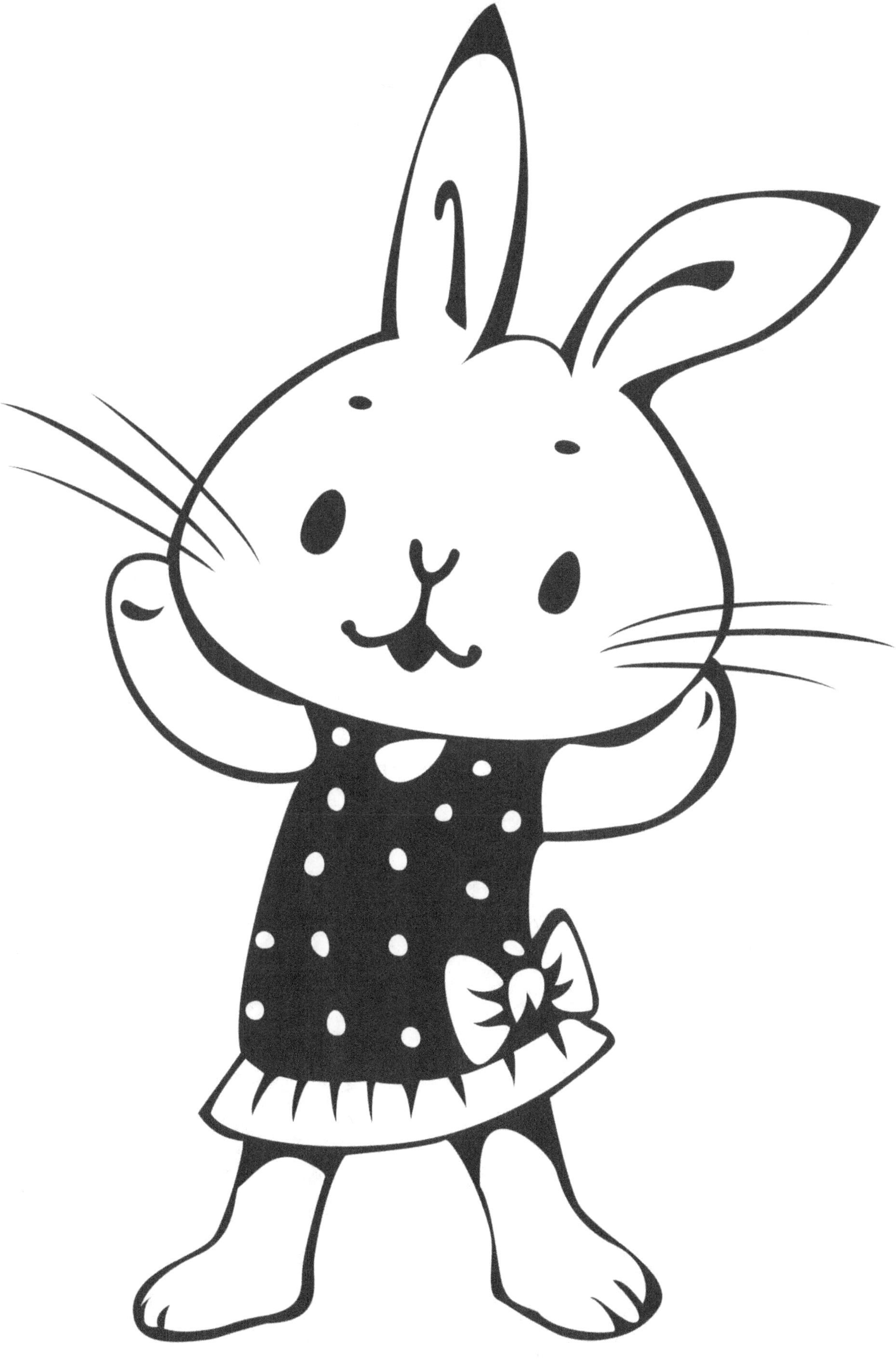

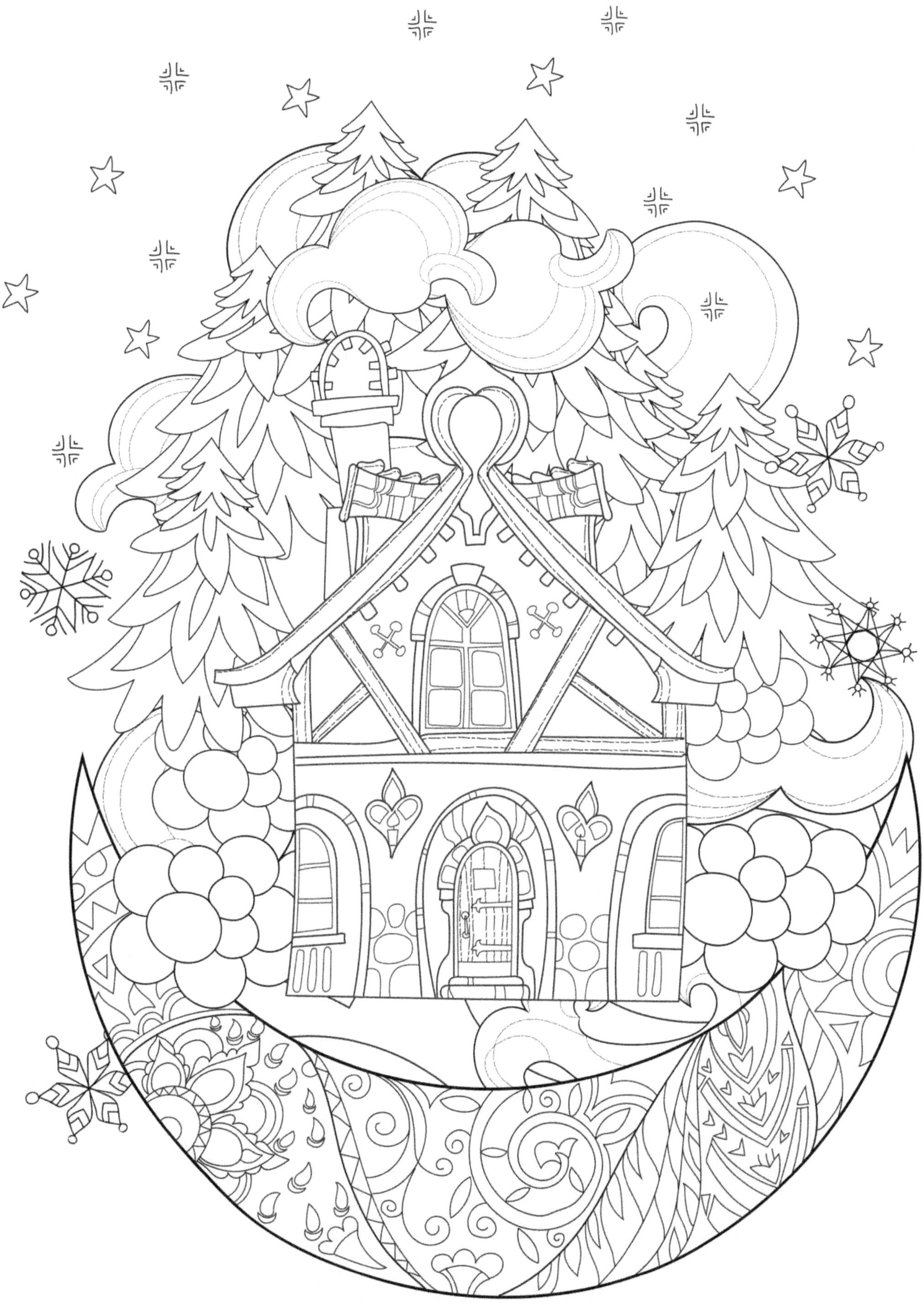

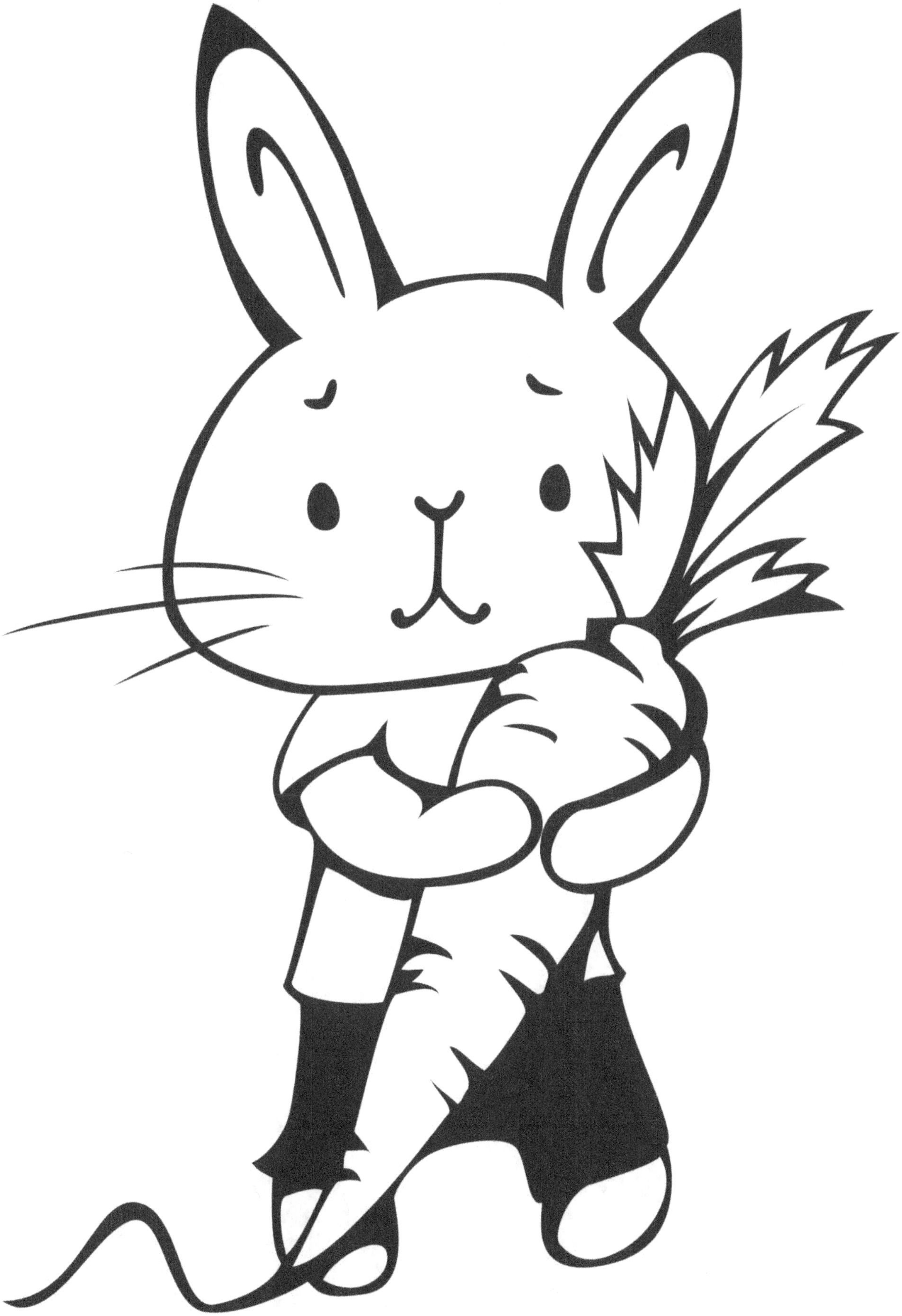

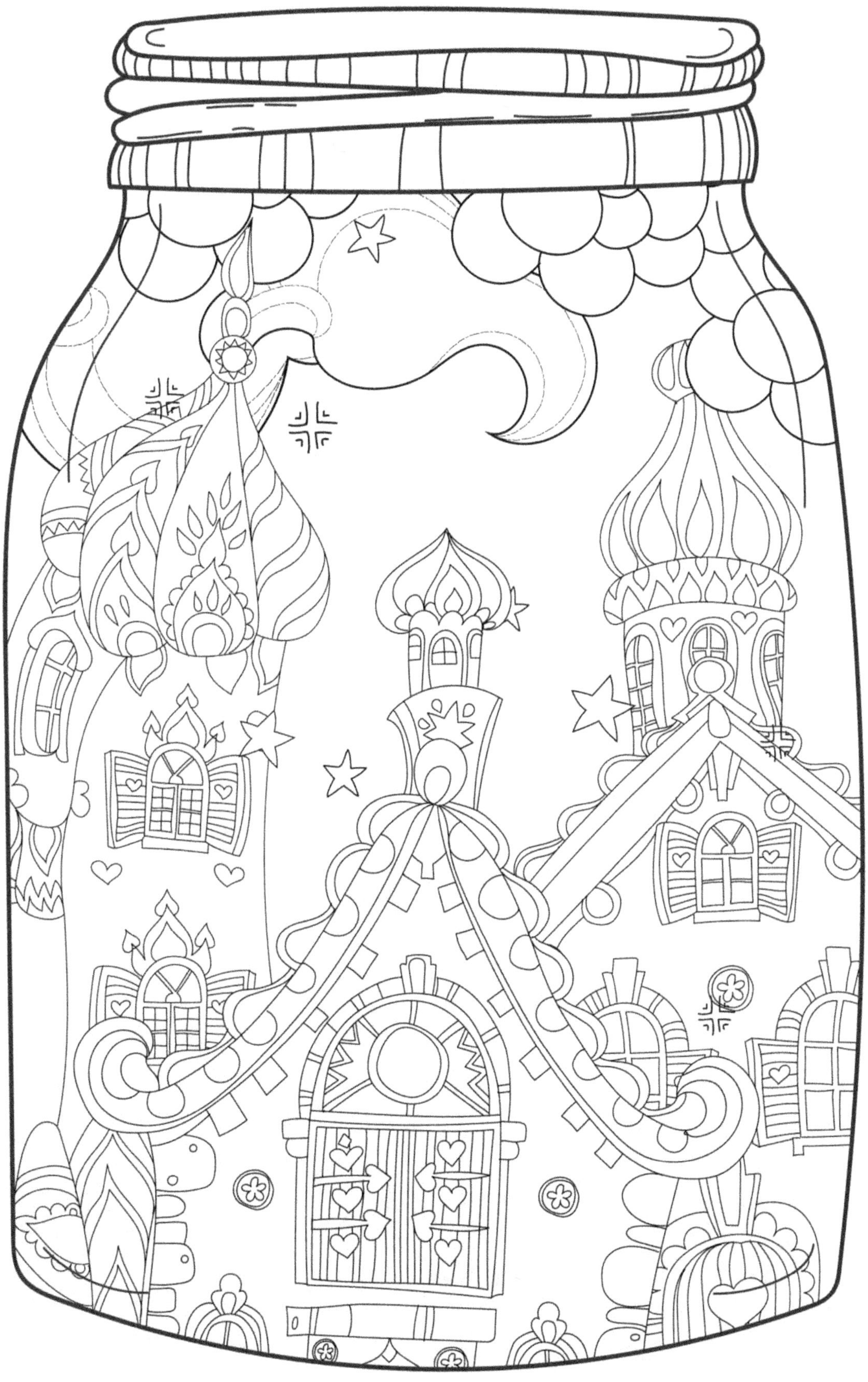

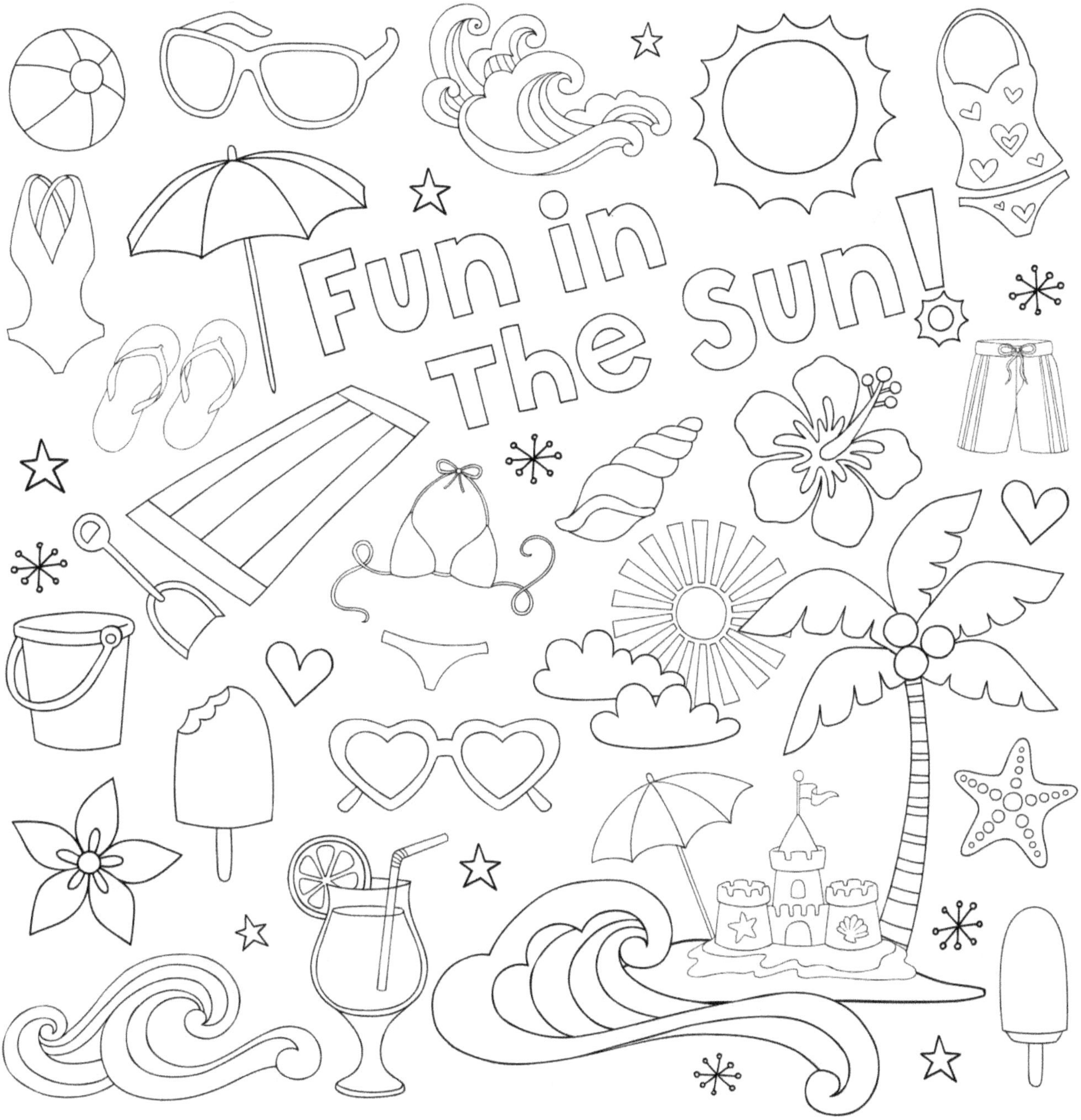
Fun in
The Sun!

www.ingramcontent.com/pod-product-compliance
Lightning Source LLC
Chambersburg PA
CBHW081600280526
45788CB00011B/3532
9781545565490